EVERYTHING I CAN BE!

Markita Richards

Illustrations by Blueberry Illustrations

This book is dedicated to all the little boys who have big dreams. Remember to always shoot for the moon but, aim for the stars because the sky is your only limit. Do all things with an intentional purpose. You are a beautiful king in the making, and one day you will make your mark on the world. Never give up!

xoxo,

Markita

TODAY, MY TEACHER GAVE MY CLASSMATES AND ME AN ASSIGNMENT.

SHE ASKED ME, JACE, WHAT WOULD YOU LIKE TO BE WHEN YOU GROW UP?

SO I STARTED TO THINK TO MYSELF, AND I WROTE DOWN WHAT I WOULD LIKE TO BE WHEN I GROW UP.

I CAN BE ANYTHING IN THE WORLD I WANT TO BE!

WHEN I SIT AND THINK ABOUT EVERYTHING I CAN BE, I GET SO EXCITED ABOUT MY FUTURE.

MY FUTURE IS BRIGHT, AND NO ONE CAN STOP MY GREATNESS BUT ME.

MANY CAREERS AND PROFESSIONS ARE WITHIN MY REACH. I WILL WORK HARD AND GO FOR WHAT IS FOR ME.

I CAN GO TO COLLEGE AND EARN A DEGREE IN EDUCATION LIKE MY TEACHER, OR EVEN GET A CULINARY ARTS DEGREE AND OPEN MY OWN RESTAURANT.

I CAN BE A CHEF AND COOK SPECIAL MEALS AND SECRET FAMILY RECIPES THAT WILL MAKE PEOPLE HAPPY.

I CAN USE MY CREATIVITY AND BE AN ENTREPRENEUR AND THE CEO OF MY OWN BUSINESS.

HOW COOL WOULD THAT BE?!

I CAN BE A JUDGE TO HELP PEOPLE WHO LOOK LIKE ME HAVE A BETTER JUDICIAL OUTCOME.

I AM VERY CURIOUS ABOUT THE WORLD AROUND ME.

BECOMING A SCIENTIST WOULD BE A GREAT WAY TO FIGURE THE WORLD OUT.

I CAN BE THE PRESIDENT OF THE UNITED STATES OF AMERICA LIKE PRESIDENT BARACK OBAMA.

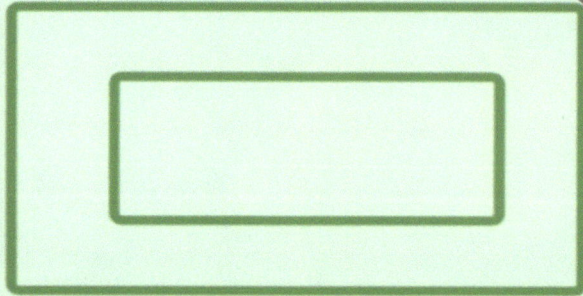

PRESIDENT JACE

MY FRIENDS AND I
CAN BE
MUSICIANS.
FANS CAN COME
AND SEE US
PERFORM.
WOULDN'T THAT BE
FUN?!

I CAN BE A DOCTOR AND MAKE PATIENTS FEEL BETTER.

DID YOU KNOW THERE ARE MANY DIFFERENT TYPES OF DOCTORS?

SUCH AS SURGEONS, DENTISTS, OR EVEN A PEDIATRICIAN THAT TAKES CARE OF KIDS LIKE ME AND YOU.

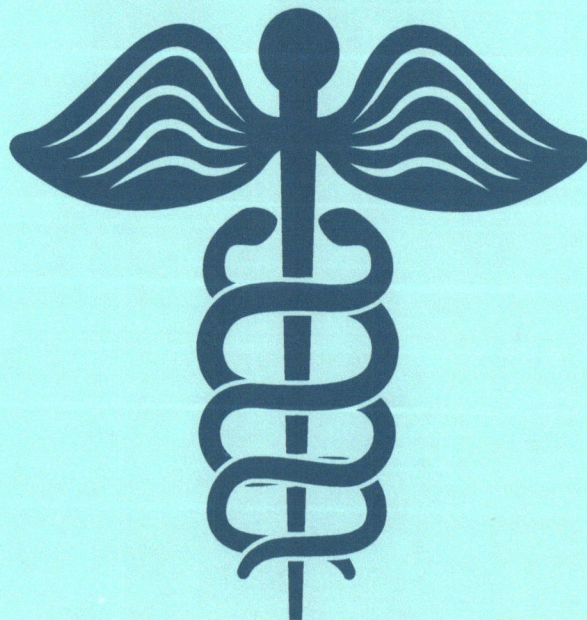

I CAN BE AN ENGINEER!

I CAN USE MY IMAGINATION AND CREATE NEW BUILDINGS FOR MY COMMUNITY.

I CAN GO AS HIGH AS THE SKY, I CAN BE A PILOT GUY! TAKING PEOPLE HERE AND THERE, I CAN FLY THEM ANYWHERE.

DO YOU KNOW WHAT A
FIREFIGHTER DOES?

THEY PUT OUT FIRES
AND SAVE LIVES.

HEROES... YEAH,
I CAN BE THAT TOO!

I CAN BE A FAMOUS ATHLETE AND PLAY BASEBALL, BASKETBALL, FOOTBALL, OR TENNIS. I CAN EVEN WORK HARD TO RUN TRACK IN THE OLYMPICS.

BASKETBALL PLAYER

ASTRONAUT

MILITARY SERVICEMAN

BASEBALL PLAYER

WHEN I GROW UP, THERE ARE MANY
THINGS I CAN BE, I WILL WORK HARD,
YOU WILL SEE!

PROFESSIONAL BOXER

FIREFIGHTER

TRACK STAR

CEO

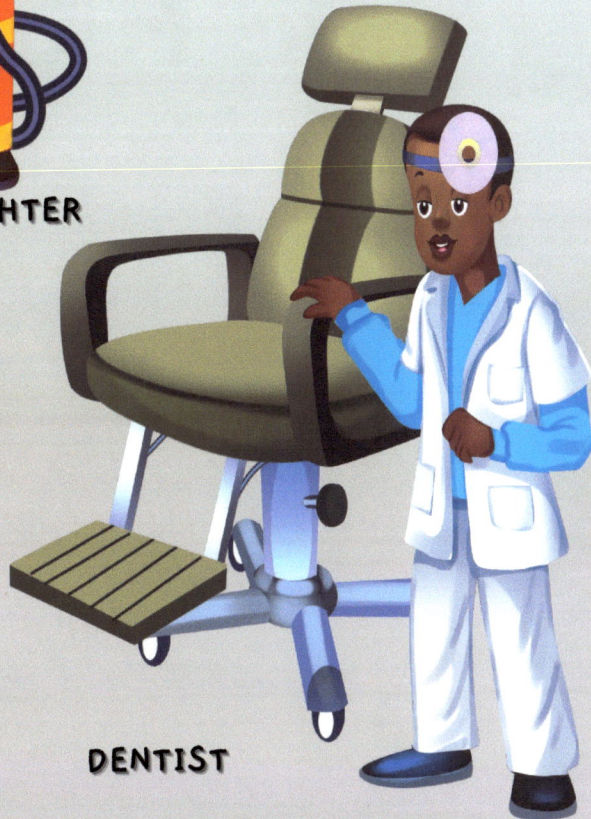

DENTIST

I CAN BE LIKE HANK AARON, WHO BROKE A LOT OF BARRIERS IN BASEBALL AND MADE HISTORY.

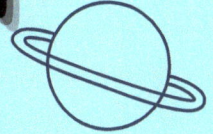

HAVE YOU EVER HEARD OF AN ASTRONAUT? ASTRONAUTS GO FAR FAR AWAY THEY TRAVEL INTO SPACE!

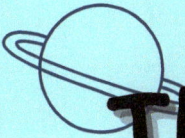

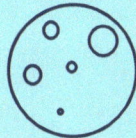

I CAN SERVE IN THE MILITARY TO HELP PROTECT THE COUNTRY AND KEEP US ALL SAFE.

I CAN BE A PROFESSIONAL BOXER AND BECOME A WORLD CHAMPION.

I CAN BE A SUPERHERO LIKE MY DAD! HE SHIELDS ME FROM HARM AND TEACHES ME RIGHT FROM WRONG. MY DAD SHOWS ME WHAT IT MEANS TO WORK HARD AND NEVER GIVE UP ON MY GOALS. MY DAD IS A REAL SUPERHERO.

Prince Jace

WHATEVER I DECIDE
TO BE WHEN I GROW
UP, I WILL WORK
HARD, DO MY BEST
AND NEVER GIVE UP
ON MY DREAMS.

Dream

PLAN

GROW

SUCCESS

HARD WORK

PERSISTENCE

LATE NIGHTS

REJECTION

SACRIFICES

DISCIPLINE

CRITICISM

DOUBTS

FAILURES

RISKS

NEVER GIVE UP!

Positive Affirmations

I AM A LEADER

I AM LOVED

I AM INTELLIGENT

I AM ME

I AM IN CHARGE OF MY EMOTIONS

I WILL NOT COMPARE MYSELF TO OTHERS

I FOCUS ON MY OWN RESULT

I AM STRONG

I WILL ALWAYS TRY MY BEST

I CHOOSE MY ATTITUDE

I AM OBEDIENT

LEARNING IS MY SUPERPOWER

I AM PERFECT JUST THE WAY I AM

I AM A HARD WORKER

I WAS BORN TO WIN

I AM BRAVE ENOUGH TO TRY

MISTAKES HELP ME LEARN AND GROW

I BELIEVE IN MYSELF

I CAN LEARN ANYTHING

QUICK GLOSSARY

A

Astronaut- a person trained to take part in space flight.

Athlete- a person who is trained in or good at games and exercises that require physical skill, endurance, and strength.

B

Business - the work a person does to earn money, a job, or trade.

Boxer-a person who fights with their fists as a sport or as a career.

C

Culinary Arts- cooking and presentation of food.

CEO-the executive with the top decision making power in an organization or business

D

Dentist-a doctor who takes care of the teeth and mouth.

E

Engineer- trained in the use or design of machines or engines or other technologies.

Entrepreneur- someone who assumes the financial risk of beginning and operating one or several businesses.

F

Firefighter-someone who fights fires.

J

Judge- a person trained to hear and decide cases brought before a court of law.

Judicial- decided in or coming from a court of law.

M

Military -groups of people that are given the power to defend the country.

Musician- a person skilled at playing, singing, or writing music.

O

Olympics -international sports.

P

Pediatrician- a doctor who takes care of babies and children.

Pilot- the operator of an aircraft.

President- and officer elected to lead a group or organization.

S

Scientist- a person who works in some branch of science.

Surgeon -a medical doctor who does surgery.

always
ALWAYS
always
Believe
IN
yourself

G **M** I Learn From My Mistake

R **I** I Will Improve by Working Hard

O **N** I Will Never Give Up on my Goals

W **D** I Am Determined to do my Best

T **S** Self-Awareness will help me succeed

H **E** I Will overcome Challenges with Effort

T I can train my Brain

About the Author

Markita Richards, born and raised in Atlanta, GA is the author of a children's book and stories on building resilience. She is a self-awareness coach and advocate. Markita holds a Master's degree in Health Psychology and believes in educating children on the importance of self-love and self-awareness. Markita writes books for children, tweens, teens, and the grown-ups they will one day become.

www.ingramcontent.com/pod-product-compliance
Lightning Source LLC
Chambersburg PA
CBHW041546040426
42447CB00002B/70